This book is due for return on or before the last date shown below.

First published in Great Britain in 1995
by Macdonald Young Books

This edition published in 2008 by Wayland,
am imprint of Hachette Children's Books

Printed in China

Wayland
338 Euston Road
London NW1 3BH

British Library Cataloguing in Publications Data available

ISBN 978 0 7502 5426 7

Wayland is a division of Hachette Children's Books,
an Hachette Livre UK Company

Geoffrey Trease

The Story of
Henry VIII

Haberdashers' Aske's
School for Girls
Junior Library

Illustrated by Pauline Hazelwood

WAYLAND

1
The Unknown Princess

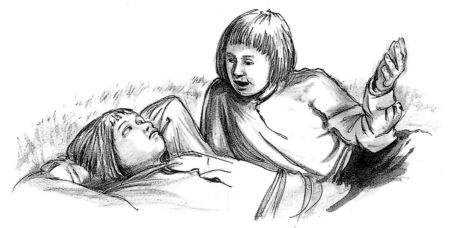

We had been fighting and fooling in the palace gardens. We lay on the grass. Dudley Collett asked, "What does your brother think?"

Harry's small eyes grew wary. "About what?"

"Having to marry a girl he's never seen! Even if she is a Spanish princess!"

"He'll do as Father says. Even princes have to."

Henry the Seventh was so strict. Harry himself had to knuckle under. He was tall and strong for his age – bigger than puny Arthur who was five years older. Harry was the natural leader in our games, not just because he was a prince but because he was the best at everything.

To the King, though, he was just a child. The King settled every detail of his life, even chose his friends. We all knew that we were hand-picked. We had the right parents, nobly born, loyal and useful.

Luckily Harry liked us. He was warm and fun-loving. His cold, grim father was often away, so life was not too serious.

Harry explained. "Arthur must marry Katherine of Aragon because we need Spain as an ally. This is how kings get allies. They marry their sons and daughters to the children of other kings."

His sister Margaret was to become Queen of Scotland. Baby Mary ended as Queen of France. Arthur would be King of England after their father. It seemed to me unfair that Harry had no glittering future. He was only the King's younger son.

2
An Important Visitor

We were always moving round the
different royal palaces, Greenwich,
Eltham, and then up-river to Richmond.

Our timetable did not change. Up
early, chapel at six, breakfast, lessons till
dinner.

Our teacher, John Skelton, was very learned but witty too … He made us laugh, but he had a big stick, and used it if we forgot our manners.

He made his own poems into songs
and sang them to us. Harry got his love
of music from Skelton and learnt to
compose it himself. He played the
recorder and the flute. By the end of
his teens he had mastered half a dozen
instruments. Harry loved to master
things.

We practised fine handwriting and studied mathematics. Skelton taught us Latin and Greek, another man took us for French. In families like ours a boy had to be fluent in French and Latin by the time he was seven.

My own Latin proved useful. One morning Skelton warned us: "You must all be on your best behaviour today. Sir Thomas More is bringing Erasmus! But the King is away, and Prince Arthur is at Ludlow, so Harry must play host. You must support him."

Dudley whispered, "Why the fuss, Will? Who's Erasmus?"

"Only about the most learned man in Europe!" I said.

Harry told me to stick by him. "I'll need you, talking to him. Your Latin's as good as mine."

Erasmus was Dutch. No one knew Dutch and he probably did not speak English. But educated people could talk in Latin.

Harry was only eight, but that day he acted with grown-up dignity.

Sir Thomas presented him with a book. I could see that Erasmus was embarrassed that he had not been warned and had himself come empty-handed.

I told Harry after they had gone. He was sorry. He liked everyone to be happy. "I must put that right," he said, and immediately wrote a letter to send after the Dutchman to put him at his ease.

Three days later Erasmus sent back
some verses he had just written and now
dedicated to the prince. I thought to
myself, Harry could have made a very
gracious king.

3
Won by a Trick

After dinner we always turned to sport.

Races and wrestling, archery, riding, jumping fences and ditches. On wet days we went to the covered tennis court.

Princes had to practise the arts of war.
Harry's father had won his crown at the
battle of Bosworth, when Richard the
Third was defeated and killed.

So we had weapon-training from
experts.

Our blunt weapons were scaled down
to match our size and strength,
everything from daggers to two-handed
swords and battle-axes. We even had
lances and charged down the lists on our
small horses, aiming at the target-rings.

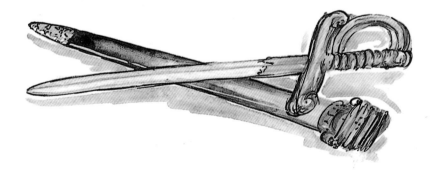

The armourers made us light-weight suits of shining armour to cover our narrow chests and skinny limbs. It was a relief on hot summer afternoons to strip off all that heavy gear and wrestle in the thinnest of vests.

I remember once – I shall not forget – beating Harry himself. As usual, he had won the first fall. He helped me up with a good-natured smile. We began to circle warily round each other again. Then we came to grips.

I had learnt a new trick from one of my father's servants, a Cornishman. I tried it.

To my delight it worked. I threw the mighty Harry. Gleefully I pressed his shoulder-blades down on the grass.

We went to it for the third and last time. His eyes were fierce as they met mine. His blood was up. In a low voice that no one else could hear he growled : "I'm going to **kill you**."

He sounded as if he meant it. But after a long minute of strain and struggle over he went again.

Dudley asked me afterwards how on earth –

"Just a Cornish trick I learnt," I told him airily.

"There's something else you'd better learn, Will Morland," he said.

"What?"

"Sometimes it's wiser not to win."

Harry and I remained good friends. But somehow I don't remember ever being asked to wrestle with him again.

4
The Girl from Spain

Arthur married Katherine of Aragon in 1499. Not properly, of course, they were both too young.

"Kings who want allies can't wait while children grow up," said Harry. "They call it a wedding by proxy."

The Spanish envoy stood in for the bride – spoke her lines and exchanged wedding-rings with Arthur.

Then they were taken to the
marriage-bed, the bed-clothes were
turned back, and the Spanish lord stuck
one fully-clothed leg between the sheets.

"Just a symbol," Harry said. We all
howled when he told us about it.

It was over a year before Katherine arrived and there could be a real wedding in St Paul's Cathedral. London was marvellously decorated.

The King was the richest monarch in Europe, but dreadfully mean. "He's splashing out for this, though," said Dudley. "Spain as an ally is worth the cost."

Katherine proved quite good-looking, fair-skinned with a red-gold tint to her hair. She was slightly older than Arthur, nearly sixteen, almost a young woman. No one could think of poor Arthur as a young man.

She was rather short, true, but half a head taller than he was. Young Harry towered over them both. That was useful, for he had to lead her to the altar in place of her father, who could not leave Spain.

At the banquet Katherine sat at the high table with the King and Queen. Arthur stayed at the young people's table. When the dancing started Katherine knew only Spanish dances, so she danced with her own ladies. Arthur found partners from the English court and circled tamely round with them.

Only Harry really enjoyed himself. He flung off his jacket and plunged with gusto into the whirling crowd.

5
And All the Trumpets Blew!

These marriage schemes were meant to lead on to a royal baby who would make a future king. But there must be patience now. The young couple were not even sharing a home yet.

Arthur went back to Ludlow Castle. Katherine stayed in London with her mother-in-law and the Queen taught her English ways. Not till December did she join Arthur.

They were fated to have only three months together. Arthur fell ill. There was an epidemic of the 'sweating sickness' in the district. The princess went down with it too.

The court was at Greenwich. A galloping courier brought the news. Arthur was dead – at only fifteen and a half.

Soon we overheard the grown-ups saying that there was no chance of his having at least left an heir. "Katherine has not started a baby," Dudley assured us. "Our Harry will be king when his father dies!"

It was an exciting thought, best spoken only in whispers.

I wondered what would happen to the poor Spanish girl. A 'widow' – at sixteen. It sounded strange. Would she go back to Spain?

"If she does," said Dudley, "the King will have to send back her dowry. All that money she brought! He won't like that." Dudley had a very practical mind.

The King had got nothing out of the deal. Spain would hardly be an ally now. If Katherine married some other prince that country would link up with Spain.

"Could be dangerous," said Dudley.

Months passed. The old courtiers muttered in corners while we wondered what Katherine's fate would be.

Then the King decided. Harry broke the news to us. "It seems best she marries **me**." He sounded quite cheerful about it. But one of the boys saw a snag.

"You can't! A man can't marry his brother's widow!"

"They reckon she was never Arthur's wife. Not properly."

"But..."

"They only went through the ceremony," said Harry. "Nothing more. They were so young."

Now he himself must wait several
years. But the future shone golden
ahead. He was now his father's certain
heir. He had been made Prince of Wales.
Destined king to be.

Just seven years after Arthur, their
father himself died quite suddenly. And
all the trumpets blew as Harry was
proclaimed, by the grace of God, King
Henry the Eighth.

6
It Was a Wonderful Party

He was never one to waste time. He had had years to think about what he would do when this day came.

His father had died on April 21, 1509. On June 3 he and Katherine were quietly married.

On June 23 – still five days short of
his eighteenth birthday – they were
crowned with splendour in Westminster
Abbey. Harry made a handsome picture
in white and gold, with gorgeous
embroideries, fairly glittering with
jewels.

I shall never forget the parties we had
in those first years. We often dressed up
and put on masks to disguise ourselves.
Once Harry made us all get up in
Lincoln green and invade the Queen's
apartments as Robin Hood and his
outlaws. Katherine and the girls had to
pretend they had no idea who we were
until we took our masks off.

Another time we wore purple satin with gold letters stuck all over us, 'H's and 'K's. We found the Queen and her ladies waiting for us with – what a surprise! – more 'H's and 'K's gold-laced to their white and green satin dresses.

People were allowed into the palace to watch us dancing. Harry liked everyone to share the fun. That evening he shouted gaily that they could move closer and, when the dances stopped, take our gold letters as keepsakes.

He could not have foreseen the wild
scramble that followed. There was such
a rush. We were like chickens being
plucked as they snatched at all those 'K's
and 'H's. Our costly satin – even the
girls' dresses – was torn to shatters.

Harry himself was stripped of his doublet and underclothes. He was left with only his shirt to cover him. But he took it in good part, and the banquet that followed was riotous with laughter.

They were wonderful times, the early years of King Harry's reign. It was a pity that they could not last for ever.

The later years were mixed with hopes and horrors, disappointments and delights. Some called him a monster. I knew he was sometimes a very unhappy man. Now I have seen his daughter crowned Queen Elizabeth. I do not think he would have been disappointed in her.